[Handwritten dedication:] To Jenny. All the best Tom Byrne 6 June 1997 Cromarty The Stables

Wolfwind

WOLFWIND ERRATA

read "Wolfwind"

oem title should read: "Commemorative Ceremony of the Knoydart Land Raid"
feat. line 5 should read: "child-choking words"
ed at the Coopers' Trade. line 24 should read: "shaking to the lathe's pounding"
sh. line 10 should read: "clenched jaw"
es. An additional last stanza:

s
id flower;
r the hard stem

ig,

. line 4 should read: "on the way to Medicine Hat."
Stoer. line 5 should read: "could complete this still-life"
read: "my great-grandmother"
read: "Commemorative Ceremony…"
line 4 should read: "bed"
elegraph Pole. line 14 should read: "in Sutherland"
Glen Shee. 8. line 3 should read: "Let her be…"
g a Salmon. line 10 should read: "time bomb"
ole. line 7 should read: "bursts from a birch tent"

for Valerie

Wolfwind

Tom Bryan

Chapman Publishing
1996

Published by
Chapman
4 Broughton Place
Edinburgh EH1 3RX
Scotland

A catalogue record for this volume is
available from the British Library.
ISBN 0-906772-63-X

Chapman New Writing Series
Editor Joy Hendry
ISSN 0953-5306

The publisher also acknowledges the financial assistance
of the Scottish Arts Council.

Some of the poems and versions of the poems have
appeared in the following magazines and anthologies:

*Assistant Librarian, Bradford Poetry Quarterly, Briggistanes,
Cencrastus, Chapman, Chester Poets* (12), *Clachan air Carn, Envoi,
Fiddlehead* (Canada), *Gairfish, Lines Review, Northwords, Period
Piece and Paperback, Plainswoman* (USA), *Scotsman* (Poem of the
Week), *Sheffield Thursday, Siud an t-Eilean* (Lewis), *Spectrum,
Tears in the Fence, Verse.*

Cover design: Fred Crayk

Printed by
Econoprint
55 Salamander Street
Leith

Contents

III Dream and Cloud

IV Alchemy

Introduction

I felt kinship with Tom Bryan before meeting him. That is because the Tom I have come to know as a person is a strong presence in his written work. Occasional poems, met in various periodicals, showed consistency of theme and style amounting to a "voice". I very much wanted to hear more of that voice and am grateful to Chapman Editions for providing this much-needed platform.

Tom Bryan does not stand alone in these pages of solid craft from which lyricism or anger can burst and be active. Here is a writer who needs to know where he has come from, but his history is more dependent on spoken references, on artefacts and skills, than it is on written ledgers.

His people had to navigate over prairies. Find subsistence crops which would flourish in environments at first alien to the growers. He has now to find strains of once-indigenous species of tree which can resist salt wind in his new territory: Stoer to Coigeach.

It's not always worthy labouring in blue dungarees. The people he quotes refuse to be blurred and so remain individuals. Their home ground is no blended moor and bracken backdrop but a startling series of specifics: adders' skins to aurora borealis.

He is fully aware of the risks of sounding dutiful. He takes them. Like Angus Martin, another poet of place and the people in it, he is also aware that these narratives of the settled – or settlers or travellers or displaced – are unconstrained. So the poems speak out to the widest community.

Ian Stephen

We call that harsh February wind the "biter"– it bites like a wolf
– it is "the wolfwind".   – a crofter

I was born in the middle of a blizzard in the middle of Canada
in the middle of February.   – T. Bryan

The ground on which we stand is sacred, holy ground. It is the
dust and blood of our ancestors... without this land, we are like
birds with broken wings.
                    – Chief Plenty Coups, Crow Indian Nation, 1909

Let us see, is this real? This life I am living? Let us see.
                                                       – Pawnee chant

You cannot harm me, you cannot harm me who has dreamed a
dream like mine.   – Ojibwa Indian song

Is duilich am fear nach bi'na chadal a dhusgadh.
– (Gaelic: It is difficult to awaken the man who is not sleeping.)

The wind is risin', blues fallin'down like hail...
                                                       – traditional blues

Acknowledgements

I would like to thank the Scottish Arts Council for a Writer's
Bursary. Also, special thanks to Ross and Cromarty District
Council for their support for a Writer-in-Residence programme
and the useful advice from the writers sponsored: Aonghas
MacNeacail, Thom Nairn and Brian McCabe.

I am grateful for the encouragement and constructive
criticism offered by the Chester Poets group, when I lived in
Chester. It was a special group of writers from many different
nationalities and backgrounds who fostered respect for one
another's efforts.

The Gaelic in "Diaspora" is taken from the song 'S fhada
leam an oidhche gheamhraidh' (popularly known as 'Faili faili
faili o ro') by the late Murdo MacFarlane of Melbost, who
worked as a young man in my native province of Manitoba
before returning to Lewis.

Finally, I would like to thank my wife Valerie and many
family and friends over the years who put up with a writer's
working habits and who offered patience and encouragement.

I Holy Ground

Holy Ground

Razor grass bled our trail
to the bluff ridge,
and from thorn jungles there,
we sought the quenching breeze.
Turning north and north again,
like forest pygmies,
we spied on air-conditioned homes
which never shimmered to the heat's command.

Child, bird, stone and tree
flung Pawnee curses
at these heaps of mortar, brick and sand.
We made treaty with bark and earth
on this God-ground,
consecrated by the Sparrow Hawk people.

and we hushed over bones and flint,
on this ravaged Mecca of dead Shwanee.
Absorbed the "learning to die" ritual
Called "Going to the Sun".

We left our childhoods on that blood-barren clay.
Thirty years later, less strong, less brave,
I could not dare that path today.

Bear Meat

We stood solemnly on cold linoleum,
fidgeting around frozen parcels
which could not be opened
until the litany of place name –
child-looking words:
Flin-Flon, Kississing, Pokatawagan.

In our childminds we imagined
burly Uncle Jack on dogsled, frosted,
blustering down gauntlets of howling wind,
cigarette stuck boldly out from the folds
of Russian parka.

The bear meat proved grey and lean.
Like stringy shanks of Sunday pork.
I alone sensed the ritual which demanded respect
for hunter and hunted, bear and bear-slayer.
I claimed the meat was good, ate until I vomited.
Ancient manhood rites fulfilled...
at the banquet table of adult deceit.

A Prairie Life (1890-1958)

I have the quilt you made
near the end of your life—
have pondered the shapes
for clues to the life behind
those high cheek bones
which blasted a thousand wrinkles
into suns of laughter.

They call this design "Dresden Plate"
each quilted flower unique,
repeating all colours,
none in the same order.
All flowers twenty petals –but one–
a quilter's tradition: deliberate imperfection
(only God is perfect).

We never knew you were sewing
a farewell, death chant for place and season.
What have you hidden in the soft pastels
of superfluous rags?
Dark signs?
Emblems of death and isolation?

Born four months to the day
before the massacre at Wounded Knee,
you remembered and told
salt leather and pungent sweat,
you were hidden from those dark riders,
broken Sioux fugitives on starving ponies–
warriors begging for corn meal and blankets.

No soft colours were ever known in Bowdle, South
Dakota.
The census reads a raw poetry:
*OCCUPATIONS: SOLDIER, WOOD CHOPPER FOR THE
ARMY, GAMBLER, SIOUX INTERPRETER.*

Army pension: SABER WOUND IN THE NECK,
RUPTURED LUNGS, SHOT THROUGH THE EYE,
LOST FINGERS TO A FELON, SCALPED,
INTERMITTENT FEVER.

Yellows, browns, blues reds...
What colour for flight, for hope?
For Saskatchewan in 1904?
For fifty years of prairie life?
Blues – the colour of strife.

People marvel at the intricacy
of your old woman's stitching,
fingers stripped and broken,
but not palsied.
Stitches closing wounds – healing stitches.

Stitch this tale:
your German-speaking Belgian father
leaving Wisconsin's plump barns
and Iowa's gentle patchwork gold
for North America's last frontier.

Blues fresh in morning birth,
reds of bloodbirth, hard wheat
yellow harvest and sunset.
Colours of prairie moon and cornflower.

This art is primitive and inscrutable.
I am reminded of Homer's ancient shield:
five-folded, earth, sun and moon,
Cities at war and at peace,
Freshly-ploughed fields,
fields rich in grain, desolate in famine.
Fat cattle, sickles and sheaf-binders,
Dancing youth, luscious vineyards,
Everything poignant, ephemeral,
Surrounded by the borders of the River of Ocean.

Perfect fusion of life and art: your quilt, your life.
Bounded by patterns of order, drudgery and hard line,
yet vibrant rippling in the wind.

If I could conjure you up from this tapestry fold,
you would laugh, pausing needle in mid-air,
You would say something like this:

"Make a poem like a quilt?
One would be enough."

Cherokee Johnny

Cherokee Johnny down our street
had both thumbs gone
and belched from a ponderous belly
which strained beneath the imprint
of turquoise belt buckle.

Drunk or sober, he slobbered down paths
too sinister for pity,
lurching his body in a tribal chant blues.
Shirtless under neon and winter moon,
he dragged his dignity
like a ball and chain.

The Poetry of the Blues

(after reading Robert Palmer's Deep Blues)

I came over on a slave ship,
Senegambia, mampata, mandingo.
I came over on a slave ship,
dega, halam, jev, walo.
Mississippi is my home,
Sunflower, Choctaw, Yazoo.
Mississippi is my home,
Indianola, Rolling Fork, Dockery's too.
Call me Pinetop, Muddy or Maceo.
Don't forget Pigmeat, Bukka or Kokomo.

Crosscut saw, prowlin' nighthawk,
Robert Johnson suits me fine.
Illinois Central and the Mobile Line.

Boogie Chillun, Mojo workin'
John Lee Hooker suits me fine,
Greyhound Bus, Sweet Home Chicago,
Highway Sixty-One, end of the line.

I Worked at the Coopers' Trade

The wheels turning my head had a soothing beauty:
blurred lines and cobweb aura of Leonardo's sketches,
dark in cool grease, enigmatic as the logic
of a medieval theologian.
Those wheels turned even smaller wheels in my head,
in mesh of grinding gears and teeth.
My dreams floated up to shafts of light
daring to enter the factory.
My thoughts flew from the cutting blade.
Cherry wood: blood-flecked,
torn from hermit hills of brooding.
Pink blossom no more to sperm the air.
This lathe rapes to uncertain beauty,
to be rubbed by callous and cynical hands.
Considered mere decoration, despised by its maker.
It won't hold bourbon –
here purpose consumes beauty.

Oak: swamp jack, mountain-man, ravine anarchist.
Says, char me, burn me, I can hold the amber fire.
can drink your molotov cocktail.
I hold fire and for it I am torn and moulded.

Ash; fickle, useless, desirable.
A flank of perfection,
sharing to the lathe's pounding,
but turning away, not made for this.
ash negated the mountain wind,
by bending Zen-like to it,
negates machine by slipping from its jaws.

Sassafras: clown, jester, death-cheater.
Green is your flag, flaunting leaves and roots.
In May you are eaten in the Cajun gumbo pot,
boiled in the swamp man's teapot.
I could not wind your vitality to cold metal,
mercurial you twitch and jump.

This lathe itself is object of an engineer's lust,
god-dynamo to purpose defined by knife
and spindle. Brain oozings from a madman.
Your magic is this: you have the Shaman power
to transform shaggy stuff made of limestone
and hard rain,
of starvation and flame-ravage
into a smooth silken thing, perfect in form,
true to purpose.
Dead, now, but more beautiful
than the life it held.

Wanderjahr

Rilke in his rucksack,
he lacked only a gingerbread house
and saintly wood-chopper
to become a stage set for
the Grimm Brothers.

Cheese and good bread by day,
wine and politics at night.
Marx by moon,
Nietzsche at noon.
Tall serious female students
whose Zeitgeist collided with his,
asked him in elided English
if they might discuss the
Categorical Imperative.

Flickering candles cast shadows
on heavy oak Teutonics
while he learned the meaning
of cool precision.

A Student in the Western Mountains

A cougar's cry
cracked the winter night
into jagged prisms,
a four-octave rabbit ripper,
a killing moan
clawing its way to the brittle moon,
an encore split the stars
into smithereens.

So cold
the killer must keep singing,
or his frozen lungs
would choke his song.

Cry of the big cat,
his pain, past proving,
on this freezing night,
we must both keep moving.

Howl

The bookshop's hostile glare
highlighted the clerk's fingers
drumming on the formica.
Friday night, closing time,
last one on the floor, I chose the book,
was ushered curtly out the door.

I read the poems home in a snowstorm,
burning a hole in my teenage brain.
It sent me on the road
while Kerouac lay bloated
in front of his mummy's TV,
ranting about the Youth of his day.

La Guerre

Our old neighbour kept bees,
amid memories of mustard gas.
He moved in cautious measure,
from house to hive, from hive to barn.
As we pitied the insomnia of his nights and days,
winter and summer
he prowled a psychic no-man's land.

Pyromania was his final solution.
His hives, greenhouse and bean rows
were sacrificed to a quenching flame,
assuaging snipers of flawless aim.
Finally, even his loyal swallows
hovered in pained circles and fled.

He survived to pace and creak,
night upon night,
until delirium dug mental trenches
deep and deeper.
He drew the curtains –
War, Reprieve, Armistice.
In his last calm days,
we saw him ready his beehives
for his exiled Queen's return.

Public Library Vignettes

1) San Francisco

The ritual: wool coats, earmuffs, scarves
steaming on whistling radiators of flaked gold.
Thermos flasks perch in perpetual near-fall.

Flotsam of Empire and Diaspora –
retired Serbian waiters and stevedores
(their faces the colour of congealed blood).
In the private Esperanto of cough and nod
chess matches last all day.

They linger proudly to closing time,
leave ceremoniously in swaddle of soggy tweed.
Outside, it is always raining.

2) Portland, Oregon

On the grass, seagulls pester vagrants for scraps,
peck angrily at empty wine bottles.
Eccentric bicycles begin to arrive,
with daffodils in the spokes.

Arrive, keepers of geese in bedsits,
Saboteurs of Public Health,
Masters of Cyrillic hoodoo,
Reciters of Russian.
(They chew tobacco,
eschew tidy lists of library "ought".)
Old Believers, Spirit Wrestlers, Fools in Christ:
all seeking asylum
in bemused halls of tolerant marble.

Car Crash

Early morning
when the corn was blistered
with fresh droplets,
dew-coated, leaves of green shellac,
still wet and rustling, rustling,
he found Danny dead,
coiled foetus-like
on the hot tar.
Two thin threads of blood
from the clenches jaw –
pencilled in like a final correction.

They took Danny's body away,
its impression left on the soft highway,
a monument lasting only
until the sun
melted the final memory
into a hot bubbling pool.

Pioneer Graveyard

I've seen how the rain works on limestone.
How it widens the letter grooves.
How pools will form.
How words melt together.
Goldfinches come for the thistles there,
while sassafras and maple roots roll stones
out into the sun.

Tiny yellow butterflies pause there
on the way to dying.

Ten Days Without Food

First, I heard the wind.
It sang but did not speak.
I saw the wind in wing of hawk.
In the leaf of birch, turning.
Then I saw God
in the blood of the panther,
in the colour of thunder.
The panther was wise (a gentle killer).
"Eat with me, brother," he said,
speaking all the dead languages of the forest.

Departures

My great-grandfather left Ireland
with hunger in his belly
and little English in his head.
The green land of Canada was his fate.
He dug its earth, was planted in it.

My grandfather and father had one thousand acres
of Saskatchewan wheat.
I have one acre of moonscape.

They would understand:
barbwire, nettles and wind.
They might even comprehend my fool's acre
of birch and rowan.

falcon, lark, come to my defence.
This living wooded earth is hard,
though softer than a landlord's heart.

II Field Of Thorns

Poetry on the Shelves

In coloured bands the words slumber,
worlds in limbo doing penance
on hard Canadian pine.
There are lives
between thin covers.
I can put my finger on Dante
or the Sound of Sleat.
In the grey confusion
of a dreich, purposeless day,
having drunk endless cups of coffee,
I cup my hands up to them,
drinking a clear spring,
a rushing mental freshet,
a fuaran out of all proportion
to the space I'm in;
a bit like growing a rowan
in a tobacco tin.

Ruined Croft

The gable gash alone is not fatal.
Slates are sliding in crazy dips,
rattling like shards in the withering wind.
Deep rivulets are eroding the bedrock.
The whole thing is sinking.
Angry armies of reeds advance,
cutting swathes
through choking daffodils.

The timber is sound.
The door ajar, but hanging.
Joists and cladding, able and dry.
For eight years, a cup of tea,
half-drunk, sits on the table.

Television; Lost in the Translation

Mindless cackle
of Aussie soaps, cockney chat,
the wonderful world of bleach,
wind-borne from Stornoway,
over the Taneras, Camas Mor, Glas-leac-Beag,
to points of ancient rock,
twisted, distorted,
sliced into clean threads of technology.
Finally, infused from gale and granite
to bring us Hollywood's
latest facelift
or cosmetic transplant.

All these wonders
teased out of a windmill
atop Meall Mor!

(note: in Strathcanaird, TV signal is powered by a windmill)

The House

(at Ach' an Dreaghainn – The Field of Thorns)

I found an Oban Times
from 1889, stuck behind the timbers.
It was placed there before
lifting the lintel stone.
He blessed the gate with a rowan.

The wood, stone and plaster,
slate and lime,
I nurture only, it is not mine.
Tell the tax man and landlord
it belongs to the wind.

I plant larch, birch and rowan
for the present and future.
I rebuild the stone wall after the gale,
knowing the gale may win.
For that reason, in the Field of Thorns,
I trim the wild rosebush.

Demolition

(for Jimmy)

In his huge hands
the rusted crowbar
was a surgical instrument.
The timbers came crisply,
the cladding slipped down in crusted layers.
Then the Zulu war shield leapt clear,
glistening black pearl
from the oyster shell of croft wall.
A brightly-feathered mask fell,
grinning wickedly in its freedom.

Gargoyle face now kissed to life
by splashing Lochaber rain.

Hemlock Tree

Needles of uneven trinity,
untidy, lank, straddling the dyke,
lone among rowan and birch,
racked by sea salt,
hail-ripped and shredded.
They say it likes shade and damp,
maybe it is a Scottish tree after all.

A man who drank your poison long ago
said know thyself – you do that well,
in a corner of hostile garden ground,
surviving more rust than green
but surviving.

Planting Potatoes During Chernobyl

The seed went in
two days before the Chernobyl Cloud
shiva-danced over the strath.
We joked about tubers
glowing in the dark.

It rained for six weeks.

The leaves grew to lovely sheen.
Tiny flowers lured bees and butterflies;
roots swelled; Edsel Blues – skins of livid heather.
Kerr's Pinks: soft carnation hue, marble-fleshed.
All perfect, as new potatoes.
Leave them for maincrop?
Eat and run?
Dig before the roots turn to slush
and cells run riot?

Let them grow.
Death and potatoes go a long way back
in my family.
Old Irish men in North America
would not risk potatoes again.
They planted maize
because the sun could cure what soil could not.

In that newer world,
death was above ground,
in the clear light of day.

Diaspora

I. Kurds in Bonn
    have molten eyes,
    huddle in Kino fronts,
    study broken pavements for clues.
    At night, in crowded flats,
    they dream of snow leopards.

II. Shasta Indians
    get drunk on the steps
    of the San Francisco Public Library.
    Their cheap sugary wine
    bleeds from broken bottles,
    drop-by-drop,
    down sewers
    where no salmon run.

III. In Wimbledon sunshine
     a giant Kerryman shakes a fist
     at the Bank of England,
     lurches between prim mothers
     in Laura Ashley frocks.
     His anger scatters the people around me –
     an Irish Moses parting a Saxon sea.

IV. Two Lewismen
    choke on a dusty highway.
    night is falling
    in the way to Medicine Hat.
    Chan' eil ceilidh air a' phreiridh...
    (there is no ceilidh on the prairie).
    Their own fathers slept in hobo boxcars
    on the Canadian Pacific,
    crammed with Blackfeet, Assiniboine and Cree.
    All seeking westwards,
    a harvest none ever found.

A Local Sentiment

Home from the trawlers
he tells white settlers to go back
where they belong. Even if I agree,
that might mean for me
claiming a piece of tarmac
on Shannon International Airport.

Funny though
his own numerous kinfolk
did not heed the same advice from
Aborigine and Maori,
Cherokee and Micmac
and where are the Picts
who can answer back?

Revolutionary Act

That azure tissue kite
claws the stairs of wind,
yearns to soar, to sever
the umbilicus of tugging hand.

Soft synthetic butterfly
can harry the harrier
and bring it down –
razor metal Goliath
and its nuclear might
brought crashing to earth
by a crepe paper kite!

(note; due to their effects on the radar of low-flying jets, kites
are not allowed to be flown above a certain height in certain
parts of the Highlands)

Larsen Crow Trap, Strath Brora

It is a cage, a trap, a crow creel.
Three living rabbits and a Judas bird.
The willing captive gorges himself
in view of his starving kin.

Crow psychology
translates his ripping beak:
he has what the tribe needs.
They descend the funnel,
become black gluttons
at a Last Supper.
Gamekeeper's club does the rest.

Meanwhile, Judas Crow
sleeps with eyes open,
eyes the rabbit warily;
wonders who did this job
before him.
Crazy crow brain bleeds an answer.
Suddenly, he has no appetite.

Crow brothers circle overhead
like vultures.

Fuaran

I carry the hoe through a hailstorm
to clean the copper filter.
Our source: ice-cube clear,
pebbles posturing as emeralds,
jasper, amethyst and pearl.
Haggard highland fence
keeps sheep carcasses at bay.
Hail ripples the surface
melting into pools
becoming tonight's cup of tea.
My job is done.
Fresh rivulets will drop from my tap
before I can walk below the burned heather.
I am working up a thirst.
Alchemy – from a tongue of silver fluxions.
It is a long walk back so my head turns over
an old blues refrain:
"I'm goin' where the water tastes like wine
goin' where the water tastes like wine."

I need go no further.

Ella (1903-1966)

Give us a four-storey tomb,
let the paint blister and strip
under pressure from gangrene walls.
No sun by day, moonlight doesn't bother.
The rooms will have floral wallpaper
of nicotine tint.
The electric fire will be the centre
of a circle within a circle
of discarded cardigans,
strewn, piled in fortress.

The electric fire warns the hungry wolves
at the perimeter: light is life.
Electric bar is a bridge of hope
to the next blossoming,
before the killing solstice.

Educated men write "hypothermia"
on Death Certificates.
(It loves grey dawn, speaks the Auld Tongue.)

John Angus

Slow treacle eyes,
pools of wisdom at the world's end.
Witch doctor, shadow hunter.
Raven vision misses nothing;
beyond the rotting village hall
he watches grazing ponies
whose riders come from Surrey and Kent.
His old school is a tearoom.
His grandfather's croft is a pottery.
Yet too proud to be bitter,
he shares out Gaelic with any
who will listen.

From further away,
his chimney can be seen
rising higher than the rest.
It is crumbling
but its vibrant smoke
rises high enough
to grapple with eagles.

Derelict Hunting Lodge, Sutherland

Floor littered with mattress stuffing,
crow feathers and sheep shit.
Brass beds sinking deep into fungal floorboards.
Three rooms where flatulent Billie Bunters –
pudgy sons of Empire drank fine malt
before dressing tomorrow's gralloch.
They left a legacy
of clay pigeon shards
and spent cartridges:
now padding for rat's nest,
baubles for crow and rook.
Pitch pine walls
totter like curtains
on a crumbling stage.
Wind and rain rehearse the final act.

Big John of Stoer

In douce Edinburgh of tidy geraniums,
his back garden was a compost heap,
with upturned boat and rusted spade
for digging new potatoes.
A prawn creel cold complete this still-life,
or a few long mackerel lines.

I saw him as often in his other world,
hauling creels in the churning
Sutherland sea.

He answered a question once,
while inspecting a rhubarb stalk.
"I speak more Gaelic in Edinburgh
than Sutherland. There are more of us here.
I speak and think in English,
I dream only in Gaelic."

CHAPMAN

Scotland's Quality
Literary Magazine

For office use only				In
N ☐	From	To		
R ☐				Proc

Subscriptions

Name..

Address ....

....

....

.... Postcode ....

Tick Subscription Rate Required:

Personal	1 year		2 years	
UK	£14		£26	
Overseas	£19		£35	
US$ Rate	$32		$59	
Institutions	1 year		2 years	
UK	£19		£35	
Overseas	£23		£42	
US$ Rate	$39		$69	

One year's subscription covers 4 issues.
Airmail outwith Europe: add £4/$7 per year

Publications & Back Issues

....

....

....

....

....

Special Chapman china mugs (£4.95 inc p&p) ....

Total ....

Please make cheques payable to *Chapman*

EDITOR
Joy Hendry

ASSOCIATE EDITOR
Robert Calder

4 Broughton Place   Edinburgh EH1 3RX   Scotland UK
Tel 0131–557 2207   Fax 0131–556 9565

Submissions are always welcome, provided they are
accompanied by return postage. Write for contributors'
guidelines to the above address.

Chapman Publications

William Souter *The Diary of a Dying Man*

Soutar's last diary, complete and unabridged, begun on learning he had TB; with marginalia, illustrations and reproductions from the original. Kept secret from his family and friends and continued until only a few hours before his death, these poignant reflections are balanced by perceptive and humorous observations. 0-906772-31-1, 64pp, £5.50

R S Silver *Conflicts and Contexts*

"Silver's poetry has both formal skill and accessibility ... an accomplished use of form, the *sine qua non* of poetic achievement." – William Neill. 0-906772-41-9, 64pp, £6.50

Hugh McMillan *Horridge*

Sometimes serene, sometimes mischievously controversial, Hugh McMillan's third collection pinpoints issues of Scottish identity and personal experience.
0-906772-52-4, 62pp £6.50

Jenny Robertson *Loss and Language*

Exploring political and linguistic loss around the world, this collection looks at women's experiences of loss, restoration and language. "Each word falls brigh and singing upon the stones of our world." — George Mackay Brown.
0-906772-62-1, 63pp, £6.50

David Purves *Herts Bluid*

Editor of Lallans magazine and active in the Scots Language Society for many years, David Purves' first collection of poetry demonstrates the depth of his love for the language with earthy humour and a shrewd eye. 0-906772-70-2, 63pp, £6.50

Alan Riach *First & Last Songs*

Strong colours, subtle music and a wry sense of humour leaven this collection of very personal poems, steeped in the intimacies of family, memory, friendship and love.
0-906772-71-0, 64pp, £8.50

George Gunn *Grey Coast & Gold of Kildonan*

Two plays, one a tragic yet hilarious and entertaining exposition of a proud, remote people trying to come to terms with forces they can no longer control; the other "steeped in legend with the natural and supernatural elements skilfully woven." – *Inverness Courier.* 0-906772-44-3, 127pp, £8.50

Ian Abbot *Avoiding the Gods*

" ... I am delighted to welcome his first book, which will release these extraordinary poems into the open air like butterflies ..."
- William Montgomerie. 0-906772-13-3, 64pp, £4.50

Anthology *Norman MacCaig: a celebration*

Produced for Norman MacCaig's eighty-fifth birthday, this anthology includes specially written for the occasion by over 90 of his writing colleagues including Ted Hughes, Seamus Heaney, Sheena Blackhall, Janice Galloway and A L Kennedy. 0-906772-74-5, 62pp, £8.00

Prices include post and packing

Selected Back Issues

Prices include post and packing

Teething pains

(my grandmother, Jessie Holland)

Married at fifteen,
child then mother.
Daughter of a Scots regiment in India,
gone native or gone,
to typhoid, malaria, dum-dum fever.

She sailed from Bombay
to become a stranger in her own land;
from the palm trees of Goa on lapping oceans.
And up from Suez,
her own child learned to walk on deck.
Cutting teeth, was given jet beads to chew upon.

My wife now has those beads
from one hundred and fifty years ago,
fossilised imprint of those first teeth,
bitten in black stone on a long journey,
to ease the pain.

Commercial Ceremony of the Knoydart Land Raid

At the Unveiling of a Memorial Cairn, 14 September, 1991

That morning, stag carcasses bled into the mud of Mallaig
pier.
Skye floated like a dead man's cloak
on a sea of shifting slag.
The boat bucked over these bad omens
into the harbour of "Knut's Fiord".
This green land, once Nazi Lord Brocket's –
bore no swastikas, only the jackboot of wind and rain.
Archie McDougall, living land raider,
strode unshaven, thirty-six years in exile,
onto the pier of his native place.
Later, at the cairn, he said little but much,
the way heroes often do.
Conifers covered the staked claims;
English is the language of pub and shop;
Their church is now a guest house.

Conifers grow quickly and die the same
but the Men of Knoydart dug an ancient soil
and planted fire.
Their war-scuffed boots planted seeds
yet growing.

Legacy

He gripped the glass, the tension eased.
He said he was only one of two men
who knew all the Gaelic names
of the Brindled Hill –
no need ever to write them down.

Every rock, gorge and meadow
necessity's index to a bleeding sheep,
troubled lambing,
adder's nest, crow's retreat.

Over a double whisky
he said he'd bequeath them to me,
knowing my stranger's interest in such things.

That was more than a few years ago
and more whisky has flowed under that bridge.
He said he is last to remember the Gaelic.

Now, I suspect he has mixed feelings
about the value of his legacy,
and probably, in truth, of me.

Two Letters from Achmore

I

The wind shrieks a heathen doctrine,
the sky is rumbling, sins abound.
Apologetic lightning sheds flamboyant fire,
thunder loosed upon the ground.
Dancing porpoises don't dance for long,
lest sea gales bring their curtain down.
Marooned seabirds from balmy lands,
curse their gaudy plumes and drown.

II

A Russian ship called *Redeemer*
dances in wide circles in obeisance to lone cormorant.
A dead rowan balances strange fruit, three crows.
Clouds clench black fingers,
clasping, then loosening, and a mountain is born.
It bursts on the day a howling ice-child
scratching the face of sun and moon,
cursing the blue-lipped kiss of morning.

Hogmanay

Innuendo and leer – the adult game.
Flushed and important with drink,
they begin to assert,
forgetting the worth of warmth
and survival of cheer.

A small boy's eyes sting from cigarette smoke.
Through the window
he sees a piece of moon rolling down a mountain.
He hears the seals of the far shore.
He alone gleans porpoise rhythms.

He will leave this room far behind
and one final mental act will do;
he pushes smoke, faces and noise
into a tightly-corked bottle
and flings it far
into his dream-splashed sea.

Good Works

She is working hard for World Peace,
Baking pies to ease Third World Dread.

(Her only child is lonely,
cries herself to sleep, is twelve, still wets the beds.)

Playschool Prophecies

Fiona will break hearts, her own heart breaking,
and dance in Paris for sagging men.

Murdo will break boats off the Coigeach,
breaking heads and bottles on the journey back.

Donnie John's brain harbours gentle snail thoughts,
he will be a failed poacher
but will ponder Orion
from the height of a snow plough.

This one will mother strong babies
in a Gaelic greening,
never forgetting the sad lights
on her grandmother's western ocean.

Defiance
Resignation
Fear
are the aura of these perfect faces.
No
smash that crystal in a million pieces,
leave their untethered limbs
to freedom's leashes!

III Dream and Cloud

With Basho on the Beinn

Ascent

Adder is a fat heather rope,
lumpish in bracken,
gliding tongue flicks for fat frog…
fat rope (frog-strangler).

Flashing frog is a wet skin glowing,
shellac and sheen of the silver rain.
Leather lizard rasps rhythm
on burnished bracken.
He is coloured like sandstone: his silent twin.

From the summit we see clouds of black ink
paint the toy-town dark,
and darken waters where mighty trawlers
seem to guddle in a child's pool.

Descent

Grass kingdoms of invisible grazers
shelter under stems
from boots bringing down panic
on microscopic civilisations.

The black mountain melts,
bound tightly by a bandage
of salt-saturated clouds.

We have walked down a floating hill,
misty fingers have lifted it beyond vision.

Level ground once more,
fat cattle road, shorn sheep;
comical chickens, snoring horses.

Windmills perk up antennae
to pluck breeze from the mountain
which has returned with the sun.

Human scale once more,
potatoes breathe under man-made mountains,
miniature, on no map painted.

Eagle on a Telegraph Pole

I sometimes see things which reason can't thole.
Alone, rising from my bothy chair,
I once saw an eagle on a telegraph pole.

The professional bird men
tell me what can not be.
But this time they can't see
the bird for the feather –
while a six-foot span
wings over the heather.

But I saw his wicked hunter's look
and I recorded him thusly in my book:

"On Saturday, Sixth of December, Nineteen Ninety-One,
I saw a bird the size of a sheep
perch on a pole n Sutherland.
He launched himself into the Elphin rain,
and flew like Icarus
into a mist-veiled sun."

A Shawnee in Glen Shee

*(a Celtic Trickster Cycle: Red Indian/
Gaelic fusion)*

1. One flower is real, the other is not.
(The real one is poisonous.)

2. Golden pebbles under falling water
are pebbles of wisdom;
dive for them, you cut your head
on the sharp rocks of the pool:
there is wisdom in bleeding, gold for a fool.

3. You may find a lover by the dark fuaran
but her kisses can drown a poor swimmer;
its water is a sweet, sweet potion.

4. Behold the sun rolling down the mountain;
chased by the moon, pursued by the sun.

5. Earthmaker made his land well,
brother trout has a place to hide.
Salmon is a silver blade.
Soft grass where hill deer dwell.

6. Rabbit, canny crafty beast,
running Ruler of the Underworld;
buzzard is grateful for your fleeing feast.

7. I was sent to Earth to clear a Path
for the coming of the People.
I built mountains on these moors,
not walls for man, but doors.

8. In order to begin the breath of Life,
Trickster must take woman for wife.
Let her ne the supple birch, swaying free –
let her shed her leaves for me.

9. Bright berries of the rowan tree,
I feel a power I can not see.
It would be wicked to cut your bark.
Hunter of evil, bringer of blessings.

10. It will be well for the men here,
let them dwell with love for each other:
Red Sister, White Brother.

11. Fasting is no good where there is no sun.
Sweat and thirst bring vision first.
On the salt-sea wind, Spirit Helper flies.
Howl wind: blow open my eyes.

12. Totem on top, Red Vision.
At the ground, licking earth – red: the colour of birth
(totem kissed by a silver breath).
Red: the colour of death.

Canoeing on Loch Veyatie, Late Summer

Slicing the trout-speckled slipstream,
over the dark silver of Veyatie,
today, a restless and turgid loch –
fifteen fathoms of darken dream.

Angry clouds choke Cul Mor;
tomb mountain on the thunder path,
the West wind troubles the white birch hills,
while green waves gash the bracken shore.

I, pilgrim, midge-eaten, soaked to the bone,
gliding a rain-pocked loch (Ice-Age born),
poet's road to the true hard North;
below, strange fish move, deep and alone.

Red Loch

Pent-up with cabin fever,
planning the route,
savouring each contour
of that improbable loch.

Hiking back to it under oily skies,
seeing skinny rowans clinging to the cliff face,
delirious stags bounding over feeder streams.
Red peat and moss
bubbling deceptive circles upwards,
sinister ripplings.

The reddish loch invites hind and stag
to drink its blood-red refraction,
where nothing waters in its sterile wash.
Acid pool with neither fish nor water boatman,
even herons do not pause there after dark.

Pike Fishing, February, Loch A'Gharbhrain

The Ice Age clawed a handful here –
five lochs gouged by a glacial fist:
Gharbhrain, na Still, Coire Lair, Prille,
and Tuath of the icy heights.

Today the sky spills
onto six floating swans
who claim the reed beds
with communal bluster.

The pool is the girth of a swelling burn,
choking under snow melt,
sponge for the lapping flood.

From there I pulled a fish
with a crocodile jaw
onto the withered heather.
Jade-banded glass,
gold-splodged gargoyle,
his carnivore's eye
glinted wickedly: simple choice –
his blood or mine.

I let it flop free,
backward, a muscled torpedo,
down, down and gone.

My memory followed him
to an identical Canadian fish
of nearly forty years ago:
to a pool of childhood – a pool like this –
Boys (like fish) need freedom to move.

The surface now blisters in the freshening wind.
Three grouse rise to rip my reverie.

While the pike has sunk to forgotten depths,
I'm reminded that memory too has sharp teeth
and jaws that dig as deep.

Hand Spawning a Salmon

Grab the beast's tail,
tuck the head under your oxter,
hand tight to the thrashing muscle.

Feel its rhythm first,
discern the mood,
work it to your own harmony,
embrace its living,
like a good set of Irish pipes.

Beware that scaled aurora borealis of flank
is a smooth-foil tome bomb,
rippling with wrist-cracking power
(and it will slap your face if you lose your place).

The fish will ease
the first eggs will drop
brightest blood-orange in your plastic pail.
It will struggle less,
will allow this rough wooing.

Life given to thousands,
this silver leaper has spent its leaping,
its skull is cracked with an oaken club.
Proud fish now a quivering, bleeding bag,
tossed into a box for catfood.

A blackbird bounces over from patient viewing,
to gobble orange eggs with orange beak.

Meanwhile the dead salmon
pales into a pale winter's day.
I grab another ripe fish –
it will go the same way.

Swallow

Sky rebel has seized the byre,
forked tail says "up yours, too".
A night singer, not for hire –
has other work to do.

Staccato zigzag is no party trick.
It covers sweeping airborne tracks,
building a nest, stick by stick,
brings broken wings and broken backs.

Nor do pretty curves strung in sky
impress flick-knife tomcat claws,
or rats who never look that high:
who etch poetry – with their jaws.

Rat Race

I saw a grey owl
perching on a lodgepole pine,
head swivelling towards A835 traffic,
preening like a sharp-taloned radar gun.

A rat scampered along the verge.
Feathered voyeur to one rat race
exploded into one of his own.
(The rats are not winning.)

IV Alchemy

Alchemy

I took two trout from the Avainn Mor,
one gorse-gold,
one smaller, silver, the colour of cold rain,
I killed the gold fish on the granite shore.

The silver one flopped bleeding to the water's edge.
With silver blade on silver gills,
I stabbed his life on the blood-soaked ledge.

I ate the trout of silver and gold,
their flesh feeding my flesh and bone.
But others I've given back to living,
by the Black Water, near the fossil stone.

Older than memory of killing there,
is the etched scroll on muted rock,
or memory scratched by eagle talon,
razor-sharp on the morning air.

I know my own time will come, the wheel must turn,
I will melt onto freezing fog,
become the wind-polished quartz.
My dead arteries will drain into the living burn.

Water wheel of life and death,
comes full circle on the Avainn Mor.
And two trout will swim again,
one gold, one silver – the colour of cold rain.

Glasgow Kebab, 1 a.m.

This is civilisation:
succulent strips of lamb
on juicy bread.
A full warm belly
primes for a winter journey
across freezing Rannoch Moor –
where sheep
munch blissfully unaware
that a spit is turning somewhere,
over brimstone
while
other bellies are being filled.

Glasgow Rush Hour

Fair and sturdy legs
at rush hour,
scramble home for warmth and tea.
Friday's cozy catlike repose.

Yet there are some on the pavement
who measure dreams only
by the thickness of cardboard
(tea and warmth are separate issues)

Rush hour river
flows around these
moss-covered rocks
in the human tide.
Boulders drowning
in a concrete current.

Cardboard is good insulation:
keeps in the cold
muffles dreams.

Invigilating School Exams

As if you could kill time without injuring Eternity.
– Thoreau

I am paid for it, the rules are clear:
no reading or writing (vigilance comes dear).
My thoughts leap through the turbulence
of the open window.
Gorse in full buzzing,
birches birling in the wind.
The future of the young is a serious affair
but my future is also my past
and memory cheats at every turn.
The pens of the pupils keep moving.
The clock ticks away.

Guidly Ballade

Soldiers stride through the village like squat tanks,
necks roughred from the sun,
pimpled with tentative tattoos,
arms swelling like sausages.

Giggling local girls
hang from the school gate
cheering and waving.

The soldiers go tomorrow,
leaving one new bridge
that should last forever.
Leaving girls whose dreams must shift
to men who will fight only in blue boiler suits
with no weapons
save spanners and diesel cans.

Travelling People, Harris, 1975

I traded bread for a tin lamp
and welcome cup of tea.
We poked the ashes of the fire,
in parley.
I trade the vineyards of California
for the salmon of the deep pool.
An old woman burst from a birch tent,
shaking her fist for tobacco.

Whispering children came forth
to bounce some laughter off
the wind and rain.
Their eyes mocking my own
which stung from
their warming fire.

Dead Horse, County Galway

I left my host sleeping
among empty beer cans
and overflowing ashtrays.
Walking out where
hard frost strangled the grass
and smoke rose in languid blocks
from gypsy caravans in the lay-by.
I felt like a simpleton from a child's book,
in a landscape where a man could yet plant a beanstalk
or trade a pig for silver.

Rounding a bend on the Dublin Road,
I saw a chestnut mare
lying dead: no blood, no wound,
no explanation.
The frost had gripped
the dripping life of its nostrils
in tiny prisms of black ice.

The Dirrie Mor Blues

The "Dirrie" – The Big Climb
leaving Garve,
you leave an outpost.
Venturing this frontier,
eyes watch in ambush:
stags foxtrot across your windscreen.

At Aultguish,
the snow swirls down and down,
and you pray your car has instinct too.
Nor does it help to think
of long-ago Hugh Mor Macgillephadruig
who once slew a horse at this exact spot
to stuff a woman and child inside
to avoid freezing to death.

I would curse
if it made the snow fall less, or the wind abate.
If flattery was potent,
I would praise the cloud and crag.

Passport: enter after darkfall,
your imagination pays the toll.

Destitution Road, Winter

This road was built on the shaky legs of famine
and the rotten haulms of potato blight.
The road to hell might be as straight,
travel the road at night,
but respect its builders.

Mind the rocks and burn in spate,
make sure your petrol tank is full.
On the Famine Road
carry enough food – just in case.

Achiltibuie Hen Yard

She described the scene,
first, to her mother in Gaelic,
then to me sixty years later;
how the hen harrier
attacked a white pigeon in the hen yard,
how the cockerel fought until
it was shredded to blood ribbons.

It drove the hawk away.
The pigeon stayed among the hens,
recovering and scratching
in the blood-soaked dust.

Bodach An Stoirm

(from Achtiltibuie, last century)

Tell me the fishermen were drunkards or liars,
describing how, windward to Tanera,
the storm shook a creature loose
which shook their boat like a herring creel.
They called their rust-red leviathan
"Old Man of the Storm."

Just a daily fact
to a Macleod or Fraser,
Sinclair or Mackenzie.
As true as a good rope,
a taut sail, or well-mended net.

Men who could read stars
could also read the depths.
They considered the poet's "Kraken"
too grand a word for a splintered keel,
a shredded net
or the ridicule their tale
met with in Stornoway.

Heron Jack

Has said nothing to no man since day one,
smokes roll-ups alone, out in the yard.
Takes his tea break out in the snow,
works shirtless in the scorching sun.

He works like only a lunatic can,
his dead down tight in a hermit's dream,
bony man, long-legged, sombre, gaunt,
looks like a heron, a heron-man.

But I've seen him watch these birds until
they vanish over the moonscape rock,
then he downs tools, work and food
and stares their flight over the bracken hill.

He then works slowly, without a word,
nods and smiles while the memory fades,
then his thoughts grow dark like the heron's night,
then his dreams plummet down like a stricken bird.

Winter Scene

Only Orion and myself
heard the Epic, scratched on ice.
A salmon leapt,
a fern sank;
we were deafened
by the genocidal footprints
of fleeing mice.

Crack

(for aonghas macneacail)

Crack is the quicksilver of song and wit,
poetry, drink and the laughter in it.

A man with hair the colour of a Tanera sunset
is singing in the corner about
the last trawl out of Grimsby
bound for the arctic fishing ground.
(Crack has been around)

More songs and stories in all tongues,
Blues and Gaelic,
from Iona to Indianola,
Manitoba to Glen Brittle,
Uig to the Isle of Dogs.
Name your sound.
(Crack has been around)

This is it:
chemistry of sight and sound,
illuminations of whisky and worse.
Council house walls transformed
to bardic hall and outlaw cave,
shelter against the yapping
of the Wolfwind.

Crack is the soul of night,
a fire at the torn fringes
of the world's hem.
Friendly farewells,
fearing neither snow nor hail,
nor the hard winter howling.

Charr

Red-fish, like me, tundra-born.
Cold-blooded northerner,
relict of the last Ice Age.

A magic name and flesh,
speared by Siberian shaman,
netted by Cree and Assiniboine,
sought in deep gorges by the Gael,
who called him "tar-ruachan" – "red belly".
Hunted by Border villages at Martinmas.

He shoals far down and deep,
in Scotland, the last of a dying race.
And so deeply he dwells
that none may know of his final going.

Raigmore Hospital, Inverness

The dawn is a raft
bobbing on a sea of mist.
It has not yet floated up
to my window.
Inside, there was no night.
Even the plumbing kept vigil.
Hypnotic hum of morning
brings fruit baskets, cups of tea,
trolleys and news
hot off the press.

An urgent helicopter
disperses the morning,
frantically unloading a patient
from somewhere west of Tir nan Og.

Scotland, 1992

Ye hard men of Highlands and Lowlands,
who fight revolutions on pub stools,
who prophesie in gruff gutturals
through pint glasses.
Who stagger boldly
to the urinal.
Proletarian Internationalists
without a nation...
Brothers unite!

If you ever sober up
and stop being hard
maybe then you'll tell me
without flaccid lies
what lives leeward
of your blood-shot eyes.
Drink Up! It's closing time!

Affirmations

After months of rain and midges,
a perfect lush plum.

The geese fly above the gale;
they always return.

Over two hundred years ago,
travellers marvelled at the marsh marigolds.
They still grow in that place.

Sleeping,
children breathe in perfect cadences.

You can dry hay on barbwire.

New potatoes boiled in mint;
harvested from between the stones.

I heard porpoises in the sea;
they were singing, not eating.

Orion is my guardian.
He keeps good hours.

The oak tree has not grown; neither has it died.

Rowans and birches flourish
where experts told me not to plant them.

Wealthy people in Paris and Vienna
pay a fortune for mushrooms
which we give away.

I have seen moths shatter light bulbs.

Rush hour Inverness
I saw a dolphin leap.

Biographical Note

Tom Bryan was born in Winnipeg, Manitoba, Canada, on 15th February 1950. His father and grandfather were wheat farmers and homesteaders near Yorkton, Saskatchewan; their forebears came to Canada from Ireland during the famine of the 1850s. His mother was a war bride from Edinburgh, with long family ties to Penicuik. Tom grew up in Winnipeg, Calgary, and later Indiana USA. He studied philosophy at the University of Idaho and Indiana University, later qualified as a librarian. He has worked a variety of jobs, including furniture maker, cooper, steeplejack, house painter and fish farmer. Travelled widely in the early 1970s when he first came to Scotland.

A widely published poet and short story writer (mainly in Scottish magazines), he has just published his first book of poems *North East Passage* (Scottish Cultural Press) and has two novels and a collection of short stories under consideration.

Tom's home is now in Strathcanaird in Wester Ross. Having left his job at a salmon farm in Sutherland, he now works full time as a journalist and writer, with help from a Scottish Arts Council Bursary (1993). Does occasional radio broadcasts on eccentric and interesting Scots who have emigrated to North America. A book on the same is looking for a publisher. Does odd jobs too. Edits Northwords literary magazine.

Tom's wife is a Scottish music teacher. They have a son and daughter. Tom is concerned with Highland land issues and crofting history, Gaelic and local history and folk music. He has planted a fair number of broadleaf trees which seem to be surviving against the odds.